VINDICATION

OF

VOLUME FIRST

OF THE

COLLECTIONS

OF

The Vermont Historical Society

FROM THE

Attacks of the New York Historical Magazine.

BY HILAND HALL.

FROM VOLUME SECOND OF THE SOCIETY'S COLLECTIONS.

MONTPELIER:
J. & J. M. POLAND'S STEAM PRESS.
1871.

VERMONT HISTORICAL SOCIETY

COLLECTIONS:

OCTAVO, TINTED PAPER, TWO VOLUMES, PUBLISHED IN 1870–71.—
VOL. I. 528 PAGES, WITH PLATES OF EIGHT VERMONT COINS;
VOL. II. 558 PAGES, WITH A PORTRAIT OF IRA ALLEN.

Price per volume,—bound in Cloth, or in Boards uncut: to Members of the Society whose fees are paid, $3—to all others $3.50. Orders filled by CHAS. REED, Montpelier.

CONTENTS OF VOL. I.

☞ See page three of cover.

VINDICATION

OF

VOLUME FIRST

OF THE

COLLECTIONS

OF

The Vermont Historical Society

FROM THE

Attacks of the New York Historical Magazine.

BY HILAND HALL.

FROM VOLUME SECOND OF THE SOCIETY'S COLLECTIONS.

MONTPELIER:
J. & J. M. POLAND'S STEAM PRESS.
1871.

VINDICATION.

In the former volume of these Collections, published in 1870, an attempt was made to embody in chronological order such authentic accounts as could be found of the proceedings of the different conventions of the inhabitants of the New Hampshire Grants, prior to the establishment of the state government of Vermont in 1778. No original journals of those conventions could be found, and information in regard to their proceedings was sought for in all quarters where it was thought it might be obtained. Among the sources from which information was procured, were the fourth volume of the Documentary History of New York, the published journals of the New York Congress of 1775, the Connecticut Courant published at Hartford for the year 1777, Mr. Slade's Vermont State Papers, the manuscript papers in the offices of the Secretaries of State at Albany and Montpelier, and a Manuscript copy, from what was believed to be an authentic copy of the journals of several conventions in 1776 and 1777. The sources from which the accounts of these proceedings were obtained were distinctly indicated in the publication itself, either by introductory statements or foot notes, so that the verification of each part, and the credit to which it was entitled, could be conveniently tested by historical students.

The number of the New York Historical Magazine for January 1871, edited by Henry B. Dawson, Esq., contains a very sharp and bitter criticism on this part of the Society's volume, in which he assumes to have discovered numerous errors and falsehoods of so flagrant a character as, in his view, to justify him in making a charge of intended deception and fraud on the part of the Committee of Publication. He claims that their work is not a fair account of actual proceedings, but is a "reconstructed record" got up by the Committee for the purpose of placing the conduct of the Vermonters in their early controversy with New York on a more favorable footing than their original proceedings would warrant, and that their publication is therefore "entirely useless as *an authority* in historical enquiry." This charge of fraud in the publication, if well founded, not only deprives it of historical authority, but ensures the just condemnation of the Committee of Publication by all lovers of honesty and truth.

The chronic propensity of Mr. Dawson to treat such opinions as do not coincide with his own, as founded in dishonesty and crime, must be well known to the readers of his magazine, and some of them may have noticed that this propensity becomes peculiarly active and violent whenever any question of Vermont history is concerned. He has in his magazine habitually sought to stigmatise Vermonters by branding them with opprobrious epithets, calling them "renegade Green Mountain Boys," "Secessionists," "Nullifiers," "traitors," "thieves," &c., &c., and it has also seemed impossible for him to notice the work of a Vermonter without, as in his present article, impugning the motives of the writer, misrepresenting his statements, and charging him with unfounded delinquencies.* This continued exhibition of his bitter hostility, together with the seriousness of his present charge against the integrity of Vermont history, must be our apology for a somewhat extended examination of the grounds on which he founds his criticisms.

Mr. Dawson commences his present strictures by stating that in their publication, the Society "employed a *copy* instead of the *original manuscripts.*" It is true that copies only were employed, and for the reason which is fully declared in their publication, that no originals could be found. Parts of the proceedings of several conventions were found in newspapers and in other publications, and in different manuscripts, as before stated, the most important of the latter being a copy of the proceedings of several conventions, furnished by the Hon. James H. Phelps, of West Townshend, Vt., which manuscript and the use made of it are particularly mentioned in the publication itself. The copy, as Judge Phelps informed the Committee, was made by him in 1852 from the back part of an old account book in which Dr. Jonas Fay, who had been clerk of some of the conventions, had made charges against his patients for medical services. The book was in the possession of Judge Phelps but a short time, and he was unable to give any certain account of what became of it, though he thought it might probably be found in the possession of some of Dr. Fay's descendants. Inquiries were made for it in quarters where it was thought most likely to be found, but without success, and it was accordingly stated (page 49) that it was "not known to be now in existence."

Mr. Dawson in his criticism undertakes to show the inaccuracy of the Society's publication by comparing it with what he calls "*the original minutes, as left by the Secretary who wrote them,*" but he does not state the form in which these "*original minutes*" have been preserved, or how or where he obtained them, or give any description of them, or specify any evidence of their authenticity. As the Society's publication shows that it was made from *copies*, because no originals could be found, and as what he claims as the original minutes must have come recently into his hands, it would seem to have been no more than fair for him to give some account of his newly discovered manuscript, before condemning others for not following it, and thus also enabling others, as well as himself, to form an opinion of what his new discovery really was, and to judge of the credit

*Hist. Mag., Vol. 10, Supplement, 199; Vol. 1, New Series, 184; Vol. 5, 345-7 and 399-401; Vol. 7, 137.

to which it was entitled. It might possibly turn out that Mr. Dawson has not in his possession "the original minutes" of any of these conventions, but only copies,—perhaps only the same book from which Judge Phelps copied,—the entries in which were certified—not as "*original minutes*," but as *copies*,—sometimes with the words "Errors excepted," as may be seen in the Society's publication at pages 13, 15, 16, 20, 34, 37, 42. But whatever may be the character of the manuscript by which Mr. Dawson calls in question the correctness of the Society's publication, it will be found on examination that several of the most important defects which he names have no existence in point of fact, and that the residue of them are so trivial and harmless as to preclude any idea, in an unprejudiced mind, that they could have been made for any sinister purpose whatever, much less for that which Mr. Dawson supposes, of enhancing the credit of Vermont at the expense of New York. In an account of some twenty different conventions held during a period of twelve years from 1765 to 1777, which covers over fifty pages of the volume and includes the names of more than two hundred different persons, many of them several times repeated, the industry of the critic has enabled him to discover three or four instances in which he claims that either the christian or surname of an individual is wrongly given, and nearly as many in which he says the day of the proper month is erroneously stated, but none of them changing the character of the proceedings in the smallest degree. These, and such like errors, which may be found in almost all publications and even in the critic's own article,—all of which would have been readily accounted for by any impartial reader, as innocent mistakes of the copyist or of the type, with other charges which are unfounded in fact,—make up his indictment against the Society for fraud in their publication.

Mr. Dawson, after stating that "a merely casual glance at the reconstructed record has satisfied us [him] that it is entirely unreliable as material for history," proceeds to specify what he terms the "more important errors, in this very important portion of the volume" of the Society, under separate and distinct heads, fourteen in number, each of which we will now proceed to notice in its order. We shall be obliged to occupy more space in the investigation than we could desire, from the necessity we feel of copying most of the critic's complaints in full, that we may not be accused of doing him injustice in stating them, as well as to exhibit to our readers the temper, or, as the lawyers would call it, the *quo animo* of his production.

We give SPECIFICATION No. 1 as near as may be, *verbatim et literatim*, as follows:

"1.—The Warrent for the first meeting, dated, according to this version, "ARLINGTON, 10th Decr. 1775" was really dated "ARLINGTON, 20th Decr. 1775;" and the third article of the same Warrent, instead of providing "To see if the Law of New York shall have free circulation where "it *doth* infringe on our properties, or Titles of Lands, or Riots (so called) "in defence of the same," as indicated in this volume, really provided "to "see if the Law of New York shall have free circulation where it *doth not* "infringe" &c. a distinction with a difference, which will be useful to those who shall study the temper of the Vermontese of that period, with due attention."

The convention, of which the notice in the warrant dated at Arlington was given, was to be holden at Dorset the 16th of January 1776, and it was certainly of no moment whatever, whether it bore date the 10th or the 20th of December, and in regard to the other supposed error complained of by Mr. Dawson, we fail to see what "the distinction with a difference" can possibly be. No question depending on the language of the article respecting "the free circulation" of the law of New York appears to have been voted upon. The convention resulted in a petition to the continental Congress, to be allowed, for the preservation of their land titles, to serve against Great Britain, under the Congress, as inhabitants of the New Hampshire Grants, and not under New York, of which petition the critic afterwards takes special notice. The omission of the word *not* in the Society's publication, if it really was an omission, was doubtless an error of the copyist or the printer, and would have been so regarded by any one not anxiously seeking a pretext for fault finding.

No. 2.—Under this specification Mr. Dawson charges that Oliver *Evits* and not Oliver *Everts* was an "assistant clerk of the convention of January 16, 1775," and that it was James *Hard* and not James *Hurd* who "served on the committee to whom the third Article in the Warr*ent* was referred." Well, it may be that Mr. Dawson is right. Both the assistant clerk and the committee man were persons unknown to fame, and it is impossible now to ascertain exactly how they wrote their names, for to this day *Everts*, *Hard* and *Hurd* are names of many families in Vermont, and *Evits* is rarely, if indeed ever, used except incorrectly for *Everts;* but what shall be thought of a critic who shall gravely found a charge of fraud against respectable persons, on the discovery of so slight a variation in the spelling of the names of two obscure individuals, who had probably been dead for more than half a century.

If we were to follow the example of the critic in cavilling at trifles, we might call his attention to errors of date and of spelling in that part of his own article already noticed, of as great significance as those he charges upon the Society's publication. Thus, in his second specification, he speaks of the meeting at Dorset of which the before mentioned notice had been given, as having been held "the 16th day of January 177*5*," when in fact it was not held till January 177*6*, one year after, which is quite as important an error as that complained of by him in the alleged change of date from the 20th to the 10th of December. Again, in his two first specifications he uses three times a word which we have not been able to find in any modern dictionary in our possession, viz. the word Warr*ent.* We suppose Mr. Dawson wrote the word Warr*ant*, with the letter *a* in the last syllable, and that the heedless typesetter changed it into an *e*, three times repeated, which makes it quite as great a blunder as the supposed change of the name of H*a*rd to H*u*rd by mistaking the letter *a* for the letter *u*. We are not so uncharitable as to charge Mr. Dawson with intentional fraud in this matter.

CHARGE NO. 3 is, that in the Petition to Congress which was adopted at the January convention of 1776 before mentioned, the order of the King in Council making Connecticut River the boundary between New York and New Hampshire was recorded in the minutes of the convention "as of the date of the *4*th of July A. D. 1764"; but that in the Society's "*reconstructed* minutes" the date is given as the *20*th of July 1764. We do not believe the date was recorded as of the 4th of July in the *original minutes*, but if it were, it was clearly a clerical mistake, which ought at once to be corrected. The official certified copy of the order which was sent out from England to Lieutenant Governor Colden, and which he published to the settlers by proclamation the 10th of April 1765, is found in the office of the Secretary of State at Albany, in volume 92 of Colonial Manuscripts at page 122. Copies of it are in the 4th volume of the Documentary History of New York at page 574; in volume 3 of Belknap's New Hampshire, page 389; and in Slade's Vermont State Papers, page 19,—all with the date of July 20, 1764. That date is also given in all histories that treat of the matter. The date of the declaration of American independence might as well be stated to have been the 20th of July, as that of the king's order to have been the *4*th of that month.

THE NEXT SPECIFICATION of Mr. Dawson is as follows:

"4.—In the same Petition and Remonstrance, reference was made, as duly recorded by the Clerk of the Convention, on the Minutes of the Convention, reference was made to the aggregate body of "Land Traders" whom the Vermontese were then resisting: in the reconstructed *Minutes*, by interpolating the words "of New York," those who have controlled the volume before us have managed to secure a new weapon for their use, in their contest with the phantoms, *from New York*, which have so long haunted them."

The words "reference was made" seem to have been *interpolated* in this specification. Should not Mr. Dawson call somebody to account for this act of *re*-construction? If the reader will examine the publication complained of, he will find that the phrase "Land Traders of New York" is used three times in the Petition, twice on page 17 and once on page 18. In the first instance, "*the Monopolizing Land Traders of New York*" are charged with being instrumental,—after the petitioners had obtained and settled on grants from New Hampshire,—in procuring the king's order of July 1764 changing their jurisdiction to New York. In the second place, that "*the Land Traders of New York Petitioned the then Governor of that Province for grants of Land,*" and obtained grants of land occupied by the petitioners. In the third instance, the petitioners speak of "*the unhappy disputes which have happened between those Land Traders of New York*" and the petitioners. The words above given in Italics are exact quotations from the petition.

The pith and substance of this complaint (No. 4) is, that by inserting the words "*of New York*" after those of "Land Traders," *one time too many*, "those who have controlled the volume" have constructed "a new weapon" with which to combat New York. It must be a sufficient answer to this complaint, that the *weapon*, whether useful or not in a fight with New York, is by no means a *new* one, but is a weapon that was in existence a long time before the Society's publication was thought of. In Slade's Vermont State Papers, published in 1823, pages 61 to 64, the Petition will be found with the words "Land Traders of New York" inserted three times precisely as in the Society's publication. The petition is also printed in the Rural Magazine, published at Rutland, by Dr. Samuel Williams, for the month of May 1795, (Vol. 1, p. 259,) with the obnoxious words "of New York" following "Land Traders" in all the places where it is found in the Society's volume. The complaint therefore of the critic, that "those who have controlled the volume before us have managed to secure a *new* weapon for their use, in their contest with the phantoms *from New York*," is altogether unfounded, the weapon being at least seventy-five years old.

It seems not a little remarkable that Mr. Dawson, who had the State Papers of Mr. Slade before him, while he was preparing his criticism, as will hereafter be seen, should have failed to look into the Petition in that volume. If he had done so he would have seen that the Society's Committee had nothing to do in constructing the supposed new weapon, and might thus have been spared *the unpleasant duty* of making a false charge against them. That he heedlessly neglected to notice so obvious a source for information on the subject, certainly cannot serve to strengthen any reputation he may now have for being a thorough and impartial searcher after historical truth.

But there could be no motive whatever for "those who controlled the volume" to insert the words *of New York* in the manner complained of, for their insertion or omission could not alter the sense of the Petition in the slightest degree. Mr. Dawson has not condescended to state in which of the three places of the Petition the words "of New York" have been *interpolated*. It could not have been where the Land Traders were first mentioned, because it would have then been indispensable to state what Land Traders were intended, and the words "of New York" would be necessarily used. It could not have been in the second instance because the words "that Province," which follow "Land Traders" in the same sentence, could refer back to no other word but "New York," which must have been previously used. It must, then, have been in regard to the third in which the offense was charged, and what is the offense? It is this, that after the term "Land Traders of New York" had been twice used in the Petition, the same Land Traders had in Mr. Dawson's manuscript been designated as "*those* Land Traders," and that the Committee had improperly added to "*those* Land Traders" the obnoxious words "of New York." Every one will readily see that "*those* Land Traders" of Mr. Dawson were the identical "Land Traders of New York" which had been previously mentioned, and that the additional words "of New York" did not and could not change the meaning of the language in the slightest degree. But if the additional words had been *newly* inserted, as charged by Mr. Dawson, the idea that they could in any way have been used as a "weapon" against New York must be set down as a mere "phantom" of the critic's own "haunted" imagination.

SPECIFICATION NO. 5 is in the following words:

"5.—The *official signatures* of the Chairman and Secretary of the Dorset Convention of the sixteenth of January, 1776, which this version of the *Minutes* presents, in the record of the same Petition and Remonstrance, at the foot of the nineteenth page of this volume, *are not in the original Minutes, as left by the Secretary who wrote them;* and, to those who are unacquainted with the facts, this strange error, of either the Editors or the Printer of this volume, will serve to destroy the usefulness of the entire entry, and to mislead those who are groping, in this dark subject, for the exact truth of the matter."

The *Italics* in this quotation, as well as the capitals, are the critic's, not ours. In making this charge, Mr. Dawson must have forgotten to take even his "merely casual glance at the teachings of this reconstructed record," with which he commenced his notice of it, for the charge is wholly without foundation in fact. The conclusion of "the Petition and Remonstrance" is, indeed, on the 19th page, but it ends with the words, "as in duty bound, your honors' petitioners shall ever pray," without any *signatures* whatever—"*official*" or otherwise. It is followed, near "the foot of the nineteenth page," by the proceedings of the convention which adopted it, which proceedings are concluded and certified towards the middle of the succeeding page. The publication, in this respect, is entirely without error. The proceedings of the convention of January 16, 1776, are given precisely as found in Slade's State Papers and in the Rural Magazine before referred to, and word for word as copied by Judge Phelps from the manuscript before described, and which is presumed to be that which is now in the possession of Mr. Dawson. We venture to say that if he will allow the Society's publication to be compared with his own manuscript, it will be found to agree with it *verbatim et literatim.*

If the absolute falsehood of this charge was not seen by Mr. Dawson, he at least made it without any examination into its truth, and with a heedlessness of the reputation of others which cannot entitle him to any special commendation as a model of historical research and fairness. He must at least be content to accept for himself the sentence he so flippantly passed upon the Editors, and admit that this "strange error" of his should "serve to destroy the usefulness" and credit of his "entire" article.

The following is the next SPECIFICATION in order:

"6.—The interpolation of a line, assigning a motive for the sudden attempt of Heman Allen to withdraw the insurgents' Petition and Remonstrance from before the Continental Congress, was simply a piece of impertinence on the part of the Editors and is a fraud on those who shall read these re-constructed *Minutes :* there is no such reason assigned, in the real Minutes, as written by the Secretary of the Convention."

Doubtless a reader of these strictures of the critic would infer from his language that the Editors he mentions had inserted in their publication certain words which did not belong there, in such a manner as to give their readers to understand that they formed a part of the original journal. They have done no such thing. They have inserted words between brackets—[thus]—as an indication that perhaps an omission had been made in the journal, which those words would supply. This practice is quite too common to deceive any one. It is indeed always understood to amount to a statement that the words thus included in brackets do *not* form a part of the text, and it is presumed that few persons other than Mr. Dawson—and he perhaps only in an emergency—would think of founding a charge of fraud upon it.

Heman Allen had been charged with the presentation of the petition of the 16th of January 1776 to Congress, and his account of his proceedings with it was entered on the journal of the convention of the 24th of July following. His statement of the withdrawal of the petition, thus entered, closed with the words, "the Petition not being ready at hand at that time," which seemed inconsistent with the fact of its withdrawal. On recurring to the journal of Congress it was found that that body, on the 4th of June 1776, passed a resolution in relation to it as follows:

"*Resolved* that Heman Allen have leave to withdraw the petition by him delivered in behalf of the inhabitants of the New Hampshire Grants, *he representing that he has left at home some papers and vouchers, necessary to support the allegations therein contained.*"

It probably occurred to the "Editors" that it was "the papers and vouchers" mentioned in the resolution of Congress, rather than the Petition, which were "not at hand," and for that reason words to such effect were inserted in brackets, when the conclusion of Mr. Allen's account would be as follows:

[Some papers and vouchers necessary to support the allegations in] "the Petition not being ready at hand at that time."

For this suggestion in brackets, reference was made to the proceedings of Congress on the subject in Slade's State Papers and the Early History of Vermont, so that every reader might know on what authority it was made and judge for himself what credit ought to be given to it. It is of very slight importance whether the suggestion be considered as entitled to credit or not. It is but a mere suggestion and certainly furnishes no ground on which to predicate a charge of fraud.

SPECIFICATION NO. 7.—In the proceedings of the Dorset convention of Sept. 25, 1776, which cover ten pages of the Society's publication, in which the names of fifty-one members and of thirty-five towns which they represented are given, Mr. Dawson has been able to find barely one grave error, and it is this, that Mr. Abraham Ives, instead of representing Wallingford, really represented N. Wallingford. He announces his important discovery of this offensive act of reconstruction in the following grave language:

"7.—In the Dorset Convention of the twenty-fifth of September, 1776, "Mr Abraham Ives" really represented "*N.* Wallingford," wherever that town may have been; not "*Wallingford*," as these re-constructed *Minutes* would have us suppose."

Well, all we can say about it is that we have heard of but one township of Wallingford in Vermont, and that in the list of members and towns of this convention in Slade's State Papers, (p. 66,) and also in a similar list in the Rural Magazine, published in 1795, (Vol. 1, 309,) Mr. Abraham Ives is made to represent Wallingford precisely as in the Society's publication, and not *N.* Wallingford. As our critic requires *N.* Wallingford to be represented, "*wherever that town may have been*," it seems he would have us suppose that Vermont was honored on that occasion by a carpet-bagger from some other state. Somewhat careless work this, for a critic in history.

The seven remaining specifications of error discovered by Mr. Dawson relate to the convention of January 15th, 1777, at which the independence of the New Hampshire Grants was declared. At the commencement of the journal of this convention as given in the Society's publication (p. 37,) it was stated that a part was taken from Slade's State Papers and the residue from the manuscript furnished by Judge Phelps. Ira Allen was the clerk of the convention, and the manuscript of Dr. Fay, from which Judge Phelps copied, does not purport to have been recorded by Dr. Fay, but to be a *copy* from that of Ira Allen, as may be seen at p. 42. Judge Phelps did not copy from Dr. Fay's manuscript that portion of the proceedings which had been printed in Slade, but made notes of the points in which he saw they varied, and from his notes a few supposed errors of the type in Slade were corrected. In a single instance, of no great importance, the text in the State Papers was preferred to the copy of Dr. Fay, for reasons which will be given hereafter.

In further proof of the supposed dishonest purposes of the Editors of the Society's publication, Mr. Dawson insists that they have made two men represent *one* town in the convention, when in reality they were the representatives of *two*—each of a separate town. This grave charge is introduced as follows:

"8.—In the Westminster Convention of January 15, 1777, this version of the *Minutes* of that body would have us believe that "Lt. Leonard Spaulding" and "Lt. Dennis Lockland" jointly represented "Dummerston," and that the town of "Putney" was not represented in that Convention, by any one: the fact is, that "Dummerston" had only *one* Delegate—"Lieut Leonard Spalding"—; that "Putney" *was* represented in the Convention; and that "Lieut Dennis Lockland" was *her* Delegate, instead of Dummerston's."

We are very glad Putney as well as Dummerston was represented in this convention. It adds to its importance by showing that a larger number of towns participated in making the declaration of independence than had been supposed. Thanks to the critic for furnishing the "Vermontese" with this "new weapon for their use in the contest with the phantoms from New York." The error in the publication was copied from Slade's State Papers, where we suppose it must have been innocently made, by either the copyist or the printer. Lest Mr. Dawson's authority be doubted, we add that in this case he has stated the fact. The Vermont Almanac and Register for 1795, printed at Windsor by Alden Spooner, confirms Mr. Dawson's statement.

SPECIFICATION NO. 9 charges that *Joseph* Williams and not "Josiah" Williams represented Pownal in this convention, which is doubtless true, as we find the name given as Major *Joseph* Williams by both Slade and Spooner. "Josiah" was a wrong reading of the manuscript copy, not chargeable to the Editors.

Mr. Dawson's next SPECIFICATION is as follows:

"10.—The re-constructed *Minutes* of the same Convention present a formal introduction of seven lines, to the Report on what is, in fact, Vermont's Declaration of Independence—certainly, as far as Vermont is concerned, an instrument of the first importance, as material for history—the original Minutes of the Convention itself, which constitute the original record of the paper, presented no such introductory matter, nor any other—our friends of the Committee to the contrary notwithstanding."

It was stated by the Committee at the commencement of the proceedings of this convention of January 1777, at page 37, that the part of the journal, which is here complained of, was copied from Slade's State Papers, and if Mr. Dawson looked into the declaration of independence as printed in that volume, he must have found those seven lines precisely as in the Society's publication. He was not a stranger to Mr. Slade's work. In his subsequent specification, No. 12, he speaks of Mr. Slade's "well known Vermont State Papers," and proceeds at once to make an important quotation from that work. The first six lines of the quotation are from the same page (69) on which the above "formal introduction" complained of is printed. We are, therefore, justified in assuming that Mr. Dawson did know, very well knew, that his proscribed introductory matter had been in print in that "well known" work for nearly fifty years. But with this knowledge he chose to treat the origin of those seven lines as a mystery, and to speak of them as if his "friends of the Committee" had surreptitiously foisted them, for some sinister purpose, into their volume. He asserts positively, that "the original minutes of the convention presented no such introductory matter." We deny his authority thus to speak. We deny that he has in his possession the *original minutes* of this convention, and therefore controvert his assertion that the introductory matter was not in the original minutes. We confidently believe it was there, and shall continue in that belief until Mr. Dawson proves the contrary by the production of the original minutes.

We suppose the manuscript, which Mr. Dawson calls the original minutes, is the book of Dr. Fay which was seen and copied by Judge Phelps as before stated. Of this convention of January 1777, Ira Allen and not Dr. Fay was the Clerk, and at the end of its proceedings in Dr. Fay's book, as copied by Judge Phelps and printed in the Society's volume, page 42, it is certified, not as the original minutes, but as "A true copy from the original."

The introductory matter complained of is in the following words:

"*To the honorable convention of representatives from the several towns on the west and east side of the range of Green Mountains, within the New-Hampshire Grants, in convention assembled:*
Your committee, to whom was referred the form of a declaration setting forth the right the inhabitants of said New Hampshire Grants have to form themselves into a separate and independent state, or government, beg leave to report, viz.:"

That these introductory words were in the report as originally made to the convention, there can be no reasonable doubt, and we think as little that they would be copied into the journal, as was the introductory matter to the report of another committee on the next page of the journal. This "formal introduction" is found in a copy of the proceedings published as long ago as 1823. It seems much more likely that they were omitted by Dr. Fay in his copy from Ira Allen's minutes, either by accident or from the belief that they might be properly left out, than that any one had undertaken to prepare them without authority to be inserted in Mr. Slade's publication. They were, indeed, merely formal, and do not alter the meaning of the proceedings in any degree whatever, and why Mr. Dawson, even if he had been ignorant of their antiquity, should undertake to magnify their insertion in the Society's volume into an offence against historical integrity, is a question which he alone can solve.

The next Charge of Reconstruction is as follows:

"11.—In the same important instrument, as originally recorded, a most important extract from the Journals of the Continental Congress, certified by the Secretary of that Congress, was introduced, as the foundation of the Convention's proposed action on that subject; in the reconstructed Minutes, the record of that resolution is changed in its terms, and the verification of the Secretary is altogether omitted—a curious and significant coincidence."

The part of the Society's work, here complained of, is copied literally from Slade's State Papers without diminution or addition, as Mr. Dawson well knew, and if it contains evidences of "reconstruction," he also knew they were of too great antiquity to be chargeable to the committee of publication. The "important extract from the Journals of the Continental Congress" is the resolution of that body of May 15, 1776, which is copied from Slade in the following words:

Resolved, That it be recommended to the respective assemblies and conventions of the United Colonies, where no government sufficient to the exigencies of their affairs, has been heretofore established, to adopt such government as shall, in the opinion of the representatives of the people, best conduce to the happiness and safety of their constituents in particular, and of America in general."

Mr. Dawson's charge is quite indefinite, but on thorough examination we are satisfied it can be no other than the discovery by him, after diligent search, that the word *heretofore* which precedes the word established, in the resolution, and which is thus copied from Slade, is printed *hitherto* in the Journal of Congress. We are unable to find any other change in the terms of the resolution. To be sure this does not make the slightest change in the meaning of the resolution, the governments which had been "*heretofore* established" being those and those only which had been "*hitherto* established." But Mr. Dawson considers this altogether harmless change made in print nearly fifty years ago, which there could never have been any motive for making, and which could not have been otherwise than accidental, as of sufficient importance to sustain a charge of a dishonest purpose in "his friends of the committee." The committee he would insinuate wickedly changed the terms of the resolution by substituting the word *heretofore* for *hitherto*, and then to soften their condemnation if detected, suppressed the Secretary's verification of the resolution, which is in Slade (77,) but *not* in the report quoted from Slade (69). These two acts, we suppose, constitute the pith and point, if there be any, of the "curious and significant coincidence" with which his charge concludes; and all this, when Mr. Dawson had full knowledge that the committee had nothing to do in originating the changes of which he complains. He must have been extremely anxious to discover an occasion for fault finding, or he could never have resorted to so flimsy a pretense for it.

CHARGE NO. 12.—Mr. Dawson in his specification No. 12 makes a quotation of some length from the declaration of independence of the New Hampshire Grants, as printed in Mr. Slade's work, which he styles Mr. Slade's "well known Vermont State Papers," to show that the new State was therein called "New Connecticut alias Vermont," and he also refers to the beforementioned manuscript, from which Judge Phelps copied, as containing the same two names, in which he is doubtless correct. In the copy in the Society's volume the words alias Vermont were omitted, and in their place were inserted two brackets, and between them was a space sufficient to contain the words, with a reference to a foot-note, thus—[[1]]—which note was as follows:

"Here in the copy in Slade's State Papers the words *alias Vermont* are inserted; but that they could not have been in the original declaration appears from the subsequent use of the name New Connecticut alone, and from the proceedings in the convention of the 4th of June following, where the name was changed to Vermont. *I. Allen's Vermont, p.* 79, and *H. Hall's Vt.*, p. 239, 297."

Mr. Dawson discovers, in this suggestion of error in the two copies of the declaration, a very great outrage. He says that both the before-mentioned copies—from Slade and Phelps—were "before the Committee when it issued this reconstructed record; and we confess," he says, "we are not acquainted with the principle which warranted the Committee, in the face of the two distinct copies of the original, to not only omit from its version of the *Minutes* the words "*alias Vermont*," but to discredit the fidelity of the only text which it employed, by doubting the existence of the words elsewhere," and he concludes his condemnation of this act of the Committee, with the sad reflection that "*Such is Vermont history, as written by Vermont historians.*" There was certainly no attempt of the Committee in this case to practice a deception in regard to the name, and whatever may be thought of the credit to which their suggestion—that the *alias Vermont* was not in the original declaration—is entitled, it is presumed there are few persons besides Mr. Dawson who will be disposed to treat it as furnishing ground for any special stigma upon Vermont or Vermont historians.

We will now proceed to give, as briefly as we can, some reasons for the belief that the words *alias Vermont* were not in the original declaration. In the language found in the Vermont State Papers and quoted by Mr. Dawson, the territory of the New Hampshire Grants "is hereby declared forever hereafter to be considered as a separate, free, and independent jurisdiction or state; by the name, and forever hereafter to be called, known and distinguished *by the name of New Connecticut, alias Vermont.*" The idea that the convention should solemnly resolve and enter on their record of the formation of a new state for all time, that it should forever thereafter have and be called by two names, or by either of two, as any and every person pleased, is, certainly, in a very high degree improbable. We suppose it more probable that the first name of the state was *New Connecticut* only, and that after the name had been changed to Vermont, the words *alias Vermont* were added by way of explanation that New Connecticut had become Vermont, and without the expectation that the added words would be treated as part of the original record. That the "alias Vermont" could not have been in the original declaration seems to be very clearly indicated by the evidence referred to in the foregoing note, which we will now introduce:

I.—The declaration was adopted by the 10th vote of the convention, after which New Connecticut is twice given in the Journal as the name of the State, and no further mention is made of Vermont,—thus:

"12th. *Voted*, That the Declaration of *New Connecticut* be inserted in the newspapers.

"13th. *Voted*, That Captain Heman Allen, Col. Thomas Chandler, and Nathan Clark, Esq., be a committee to prepare the Declaration for the Press as soon as may be.

"14th. *Voted*, That Doct. Jonas Fay, Col. Thomas Chittenden, Doct. Reuben Jones, Col. Jacob Bailey and Capt. Heman Allen be the Delegates to carry the Remonstrance and Petition to the Hon. Continental Congress and further to negotiate business in behalf of *New Connecticut*."—*Vt. Hist. Collections*, vol. 1, p. 41.

II.—The revised declaration, as prepared for the press in pursuance of the 13th vote of the convention, was published in the Connecticut *Courant* for March 17, 1777, which revised declaration concludes in these words, "The said State hereafter to be called by the name of *New Connecticut*."—*Ibid*, p. 47.

III.—The January convention of 1777 adjourned to meet at Windsor the 4th day of the following June. The proceedings of this convention commence as follows:

"NEW HAMPSHIRE GRANTS *(alias)*
NEW CONNECTICUT; } Windsor, June 4th, 1777.

"Convention opened according to adjournment," &c.—*Ibid*, p. 48.

The following are extracts from the Journal of the further proceedings of this convention; which were altogether inconsistent with the supposition that the name *Vermont* could have been in any way used at its previous meeting:

"STATE OF VERMONT,
In General Convention, Windsor, June 4, 1777. }

"*Whereas* this convention did at their session in Westminster, the 15th day of January last, among other things declare the district of land commonly called and known by the name of the New Hampshire Grants to be "a free and independent state capable of regulating their own internal police in all and every respect whatsoever, and *that it should thereafter be known by the name of New Connecticut:* * * * * * * * and *Whereas*, this convention have been informed that a district of land lying on the Susquehanna river, has been heretofore and is now known by the name of New Connecticut, which was unknown to them until sometime since the declaration at Westminster aforesaid; and as it would be inconvenient in many respects for two separate districts on this continent to have the same name:

Resolved, Therefore, unanimously, that the said district described in the preamble to the declaration at Westminster, aforesaid, shall now hereafter be called and known by the name of VERMONT."—*Ibid*, p. 50.

Afterwards at the same convention the question was proposed whether the members would proceed to business on the former declaration at Westminster, "with this alteration only, *that instead of New Connecticut the said district should ever be known by the name of* VERMONT," and it was voted by the seventy-one members present in the affirmative.—*Ibid*, p. 51.

The official proceedings of these two conventions, of January and June 1777, seem conclusively to show that the first name given to the state must have been *New Connecticut* only, and that afterwards the name VERMONT was substituted for it.

IV.—Further, Ira Allen, who, as we have seen, was clerk of the January convention at which this declaration of independence was made, gives in his History of Vermont the substance of it in nearly the same language as it is in Slade's State Papers, in which it is declared that the state is "to be forever hereafter called, known and distinguished by the name of *New Connecticut*," without any mention of Vermont. Mr. Allen also afterwards says that the name *Vermont* was given to the State by Dr. Thomas Young of Philadelphia, and that the delegates of the January convention, who had been appointed to present their declaration to the Continental Congress,—"Fay, Chittenden, Allen and Jones,—returned from Congress, without the decision of that body on their petition in behalf of the inhabitants, and brought with them Dr. Young's letter printed and published at Philadelphia, addressed to the inhabitants of VERMONT."—*Allen's Vt.*, 79, 86, and *Vt. Hist. Collections*, vol. 1, 375, 379.

The true history of the change of name is doubtless the following: When the delegates arrived at Philadelphia they learned that the name New Connecticut had already been appropriated for another territory, and saw the necessity of changing it. On consultation with Dr. Young they approved of his recommendation of the name *Vermont*, and agreed to favor its adoption. In their petition to Congress, which was presented the 8th of April 1777, they did not therefore mention any name for their new state. Doct. Young's letter, with which they returned to Vermont, bore date the 11th of April 1777. All the delegates were members of the following June convention, and participated in making the change of the name of the state from New Connecticut to Vermont agreeably to their previous understanding with Dr. Young.

We have perhaps occupied more space in the consideration of this question than it deserved. It has nothing whatever to do with the old controversy between New York and Vermont, for as regarded that, the name assumed by the new state was quite immaterial. We are unable to account for Mr. Dawson's hot indignation at the innocent suggestion of the committee of publication in this matter, but upon the supposition — which indeed derives support from what he has long been attempting — that he considers himself engaged in a mission to discredit and condemn all Vermont history whatever.

We trust sufficient evidence has been adduced to show that the suggestion that the first name of the new state was New Connecticut, without an *alias*, was not rashly and inconsiderately made.

Mr. Dawson's 13th COMPLAINT is as follows:

"13.—The latter part of the Report or Declaration of Vermont's Independence, is so perfectly muddled—there are not less than five serious errors, affecting the sense, within the last six lines—that no one except an expert in Vermont history, can possibly understand it accurately."

The language in the Society's volume is the same as in Slade's State Papers, and as we are unable to discover the "five serious errors" spoken of, we pass over this specification without further notice.

The final crushing CHARGE OF RECONSTRUCTION is as follows:

"14.—Messrs. John Sessions and *Simeon* Stephens were the two Representatives from Cumberland County, in the convention of the State of New York, whom the insurgents in Vermont directed to withdraw from that body; Messrs. John Sessions and *Simon* Stephens, are said in this reconstructed record, to have thus officiated as such Representatives, in the Legislature of New York, of which State Vermont was then a part."

We take issue with Mr. Dawson and say, that *Simeon* Stephens was *not* a member of the New York Convention, as asserted by him, but that *Simon* Stephens (or rather Simon *Stevens*, as the latter name was usually spelled,) *was*. And for proof we refer him to volume 1, page 515, of the Journal of the New York Convention published at Albany in 1842, where in the Journal for July 9, 1776, he will find the following entries, viz.:

"The Deputies from Cumberland county attending, produced a certificate, signed by James Clay, chairman of the county committee, and dated at Westminster the 28th of June last; whereby it appears that Colo. Joseph Marsh, *Simon* Stevens and John Sessions, have been duly elected to represent said County in this Congress, and invested with full powers of legislation, &c.
Ordered, That the Deputies from Cumberland county take their seats."

It appears also from B. H. Hall's History of Eastern Vermont, pages 258, 263 and 787, that *Simon* and not Simeon Stevens was the delegate to the New York convention, whom the Vermont convention of January 1777 "directed to withdraw from that body." B. H. Hall gave many particulars in the life of *Simon* Stevens, and among them his residence in Springfield. *Simon* Stevens represented Springfield in the Vermont State Convention of January 1791, which adopted the Constitution of the United States. The delegates signed the resolution of adoption, and the original paper, *with the autograph of Simon Stevens*, is in the possession of one of the "Editors" of the Society's publication. So much for the overweening confidence of Mr. Dawson in *Simeon* Stephens, and in his own infallibility.

We have now gone through with the examination of all the evidence brought forward by Mr. Dawson to fasten upon the Vermont Historical Society the charge of undertaking to impose upon the public a false and fraudulent account of the early proceedings of the people of their state, in order, as he would have his readers believe, that their conduct towards the government of New York, in their ancient controversy, might appear in a more favorable light than the facts as they really existed would warrant. We have seen that he has utterly failed to adduce a particle of proof to sustain the charge ; that the most important of the changes alleged by him to have been made from what he calls " the original record," have no existence in point of fact, and that the residue are so trifling and insignificant as to preclude any supposition that they could have been made for any sinister purpose whatever, consisting of such changes as the substitution of one vowel for another in the spelling of the first or second name of some unknown person ; by the use of one figure for another in a date of the month, or the omission or the insertion of an unimportant or synonimous word, which makes no alteration in the meaning — all of which changes any unprejudiced reader, if he noticed them, would at once have set down as accidental errors of the copyist or of the type — such errors indeed as an industrious critic might find in the most carefully prepared work — such as are, in fact, found in Mr. Dawson's own criticism quite as frequently as in the pages of the Society's publication which he condemns.

The hostile temper of Mr. Dawson towards " the Vermontese," and his predetermination to find something to complain of against them, are as clearly exhibited in the language of his criticism, as its destitution of facts to sustain it is shown to have been. The standing program of his Magazine, which is printed on its covers, states that it will contain, among other things, " *Carefully prepared and impartial* notices of *New Books* and Engravings, especially those relating to the *History*, Antiquities or Biography, of *America*." If his present article on the volume of the Vermont Historical Collections is to be taken as a fair specimen of his " carefully prepared and impartial notices of new books, " the aid to be expected from this department of his Magazine in the elucidation of American history cannot be very great.

After the full exposure which has been made of the fallacy of Mr Dawson's criticism, it may be pleasant to read his concluding tirade against Vermont history and Vermont historians. It is as follows :

" There are many other errors which we have not space enough to allude to ; but we have said enough to show how entirely useless this portion of the volume is, as *an authority* in historical inquiry. It may serve the purpose for which it was probably intended among those who read the history of Vermont from the Vermontese stand-point ; but to those who read history for the purpose of ascertaining what the truth is concerning those, within the recognized territory of New York, who refused obedience to the laws and public officers of the state of which they openly professed to be citizens — of those in fact, who led all others in the grave offence of secession from a recognized government, exercising legal and publicly-recognized authority over them, some other authority will be requisite. These, probably, will not be contented with either Vermont history or Vermont historians, as the former is now written, and as the latter now write. "

This is not a proper occasion for discussing with Mr. Dawson the merits of the old controversy between Vermont and New York, which ended in the acknowledgement of the independence of the former by the latter. Mr. Dawson, as often as he has taken occasion to assail Vermonters and Vermont history, has never got beyond the argument that is implied in the above paragraph, that the Vermonters were criminally wrong, because they "refused obedience to the laws and public officers of the state of which they openly professed to be citizens." It does not seem ever to have occurred to him that there might be an important question beyond *that*, viz.: *Whether the actual and threatened oppressions of the New York government were not such as to justify their disobedience?* He does not appear to see that this question arises in the case of New York against Vermont precisely as it did between Great Britain and her colonies, and that Vermonters did not, as he states, take the lead of "all others in the grave offence of secession from a recognized government, exercising legal and publicly-recognized authority over them," but only followed the example and lead of the American colonies in their secession from Great Britain,—the secession of the colonies having taken place July 4, 1776, while that of Vermont did not occur until the following January. In this and such like condemnation of the Vermonters, he merely repeats the argument of the old English Tories against the colonists, who equally with the Vermonters had refused obedience to the laws of a "recognized government" to which they acknowledged themselves to be legally subjected. If Mr. Dawson should ever get beyond the point of calling the Vermonters hard names, and should undertake to show that the conduct of the New York government, in endeavoring to deprive the Vermont settlers of the lands they had honestly purchased and improved, for the benefit of a set of New York city speculators, was right and just, and ought to have been submitted to, we shall be glad to see his evidence and read his argument. We are inclined to think he would find it rather an ugly business, and that he will not venture upon it.

We are well aware that in any controversy with the Editor of the Historical Magazine, we Vermonters stand on greatly unequal terms. His article is extensively circulated through the country, while this refutation of it will be seen by comparatively few persons. His hitherto unceasing hostility is not likely to be conciliated by this expose of the injustice and absurdity of his attacks, and we may expect a continuance of them, with perhaps increased violence. We shall probably be content to rest under any further imputations he may cast upon us, without reply. His seemingly uncontrollable propensity to impugn the motives and assail the integrity, as well as to misrepresent the conduct and arguments of those who fail to concur in his opinions and share his antipathies, must be well known to his readers, and we confidently trust they will be prepared to make due allowance for this unhappy weakness of his, and will estimate what he may say at just about its actual value.

VERMONT HISTORICAL SOCIETY
COLLECTIONS.

CONTENTS OF VOL. II.

VERMONT HISTORICAL SOCIETY.

OFFICERS OCTOBER 1870 TO OCTOBER 1872.

PRESIDENT,
REV. WILLIAM H. LORD, D. D., Montpelier.

VICE PRESIDENTS,
HON. JAMES BARRETT, Woodstock,
HON. LOYAL C. KELLOGG, Benson,
REV. ROGER S. HOWARD, D. D., Northfield.

RECORDING SECRETARY,
HENRY CLARK, ESQ., Rutland.

CORRESPONDING SECRETARY,
HON. GEORGE G. BENEDICT, Burlington.

TREASURER,
COL. HERMON D. HOPKINS, Montpelier.

LIBRARIAN,
HON. CHARLES REED, Montpelier.

BOARD OF CURATORS,
HON. GEORGE NICHOLS, Northfield, } *Ex Officio.*
HON. WHITMAN G. FERRIN, Montpelier, } *Ex Officio.*
HON. CHARLES REED, Montpelier, } *Ex Officio.*
DR. P. D. BRADFORD, Northfield,
REV. CHARLES S. SMITH, Montpelier,
HON. JOHN R. CLEAVELAND, Brookfield,
ORVILLE S. BLISS, ESQ., Georgia,
HON. RUSSELL S. TAFT, Burlington,
COL. FRANKLIN FAIRBANKS, St. Johnsbury.

STANDING COMMITTEES.

Printing and Publishing.—Messrs. HILAND HALL, North Bennington; CHARLES REED, and ELIAKIM P. WALTON, Montpelier.

On the Library and Cabinet.—Messrs. ROGER S. HOWARD, Northfield; CHARLES S. SMITH, Montpelier; RUSSELL S. TAFT, Burlington.

On Finance.—Messrs. CHARLES DEWEY, and CHARLES REED, Montpelier; FRANKLIN FAIRBANKS, St. Johnsbury.

☞Donations of Manuscripts, Books, Pamphlets, Newspapers, &c., should be addressed to CHARLES REED, Librarian, Montpelier.

www.ingramcontent.com/pod-product-compliance
Lightning Source LLC
LaVergne TN
LVHW011145110826
845150LV00008B/2530